NATIONAL GEOGRAPHIC
KIDS

EVERYTHING
BIG CATS

NATIONAL GEOGRAPHIC

NATIONAL GEOGRAPHIC
KIDS

EVERYTHING BIG CATS

BY ELIZABETH CARNEY

NATIONAL GEOGRAPHIC

WASHINGTON, D.C.

CONTENTS

A lioness and her cubs take a cool drink from a watering hole in Serengeti National Park.

A female tiger, or tigress, sneaks up on a potential meal.

INTRODUCTION

KINGS OF THE JUNGLE.
GHOSTS OF THE SAVANNA. RULERS OF THE RAIN FOREST. No matter where they're found, the world's big cats command titles of respect and awe. A fearsome foursome—lions, tigers, jaguars, and leopards—makes up the feline family's roster of heavyweights. With powerful, streamlined bodies built for killing, these cats sit at the top of their ecosystems' food chains.

Nothing comes easily to some of nature's most feared predators, however. Experts worry that some big cats are running down the last of their "nine lives." How did these mighty cats find themselves scratching at extinction's door? And what makes them so special? Let's find out EVERYTHING about big cats!

EXPLORERS' CORNER

Hi! We're Beverly and Dereck Joubert.

We've spent more than 25 years studying, filming, and photographing big cats. We can read a big cat's twitch of the tail or curl of the lip and know whether it's just playing or ready to charge. When you see us, we'll share our experiences with big cats in the wild. Look for this Explorers' Corner, and you'll be one step closer to being a big cat expert.

A leopard bounds through the grass in the Masai Mara National Reserve in Kenya.

BRING ON THE BIG CATS

A young male jaguar drools in anticipation of a meal.

CATNIP AN ADULT LION'S ROAR CAN BE HEARD UP TO 5 MILES (8 KILOMETERS) AWAY.

WHAT'S A BIG CAT?

JAGUARS

PEOPLE MIGHT CONSIDER YOUR NEIGHBOR'S 25-POUND TABBY A "BIG CAT," BUT TO WILDLIFE EXPERTS, THE TERM HAS A SPECIFIC MEANING. Big cats are often defined as the four living members of the genus Panthera: tigers, lions, leopards, and jaguars. These cats have the ability to roar. They cannot purr the way house cats do. Big cats can only make a purring noise while breathing out.

All big cats are carnivores, which means they survive solely on the flesh of other animals. To do this, they have adaptations that make them excellent hunters, like powerful jaws, long, sharp claws, and dagger-like teeth. All big cats need a lot of land to roam and abundant prey to hunt.

LEOPARDS

TIGERS

LIONS

WHO'S WHO?

BIG CATS MAY HAVE A LOT OF FEATURES IN COMMON, BUT IF YOU KNOW WHAT TO LOOK FOR, YOU'LL BE ABLE TO TELL WHO'S WHO IN NO TIME.

FUR

JAGUARS

A jaguar's coat pattern looks similar to that of a leopard. Both have dark spots called rosettes, but there's a way to spot the difference. Jaguars' rosettes have irregularly shaped borders and at least one black dot in the center.

TIGERS

Most tigers are orange-colored with vertical black stripes on their bodies. This coloring helps the cats blend in with tall grasses as they sneak up on prey. Tigers are the only big cats that have stripes. These markings are like fingerprints; no two stripe patterns are alike.

LEOPARDS

A leopard's yellowy coat has dark spots called rosettes on its back and sides. In leopards, the rosettes' edges are smooth and circular. This color combo helps leopards blend into their surroundings.

LIONS

Lions have a light brown, or tawny, coat and a tuft of black hair at the end of their tails. When they reach their prime, most male lions have shaggy manes that help males look larger and more intimidating. Scientists have found that female lions prefer males with long, dark manes.

CATNIP JAGUARS AND TIGERS LOVE TO GO FOR A SWIM. THEY ARE TWO OF THE FEW CAT SPECIES THAT ENJOY WATER.

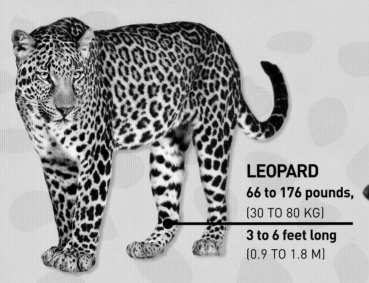

LEOPARD
66 to 176 pounds,
(30 TO 80 KG)

3 to 6 feet long
(0.9 TO 1.8 M)

Siberian, or Amur, tigers hold the title for biggest of the big cats. They can weigh up to 660 pounds and be as long as a station wagon. Leopards are the smallest, but they're no house cats. They weigh up to 176 pounds and measure up to six feet in length.

JAGUAR
70 to 300 pounds
(32 TO 136 KG)

3.8 to 6 feet long
(1.2 TO 1.8 M)

TIGER
200 to 660 pounds
(90 TO 300 KG)

7 to 13 feet long
(2.1 TO 4 M)

LION
265 to 420 pounds
(122 TO 191 KG)

4.6 to 8.3 feet long
(1.4 TO 2.5 M)

WHAT ABOUT BLACK PANTHERS?

These black beauties are actually either jaguars or leopards, just darkly dressed. "Black panther" is a term for a black-colored big cat. It isn't a separate animal. Both black jaguars and black leopards still have spots; they're just harder to see within their dark fur. A black coat comes from a specific combination of genes inherited from a cat's parents. In the wild, black jaguars are more common than black leopards.

WHERE TO FIND BIG CATS

BIG CATS CAN BE FOUND AROUND THE WORLD **IN MANY TYPES OF HABITATS** and climates. Tigers can be found the farthest north, with one type inhabiting the snow-covered forests of Siberia. Jaguars favor the steamy rain forests and sunny grasslands of Central and South America. Lions primarily prowl the plains of central and southern Africa. Leopards—the most widespread of all the big cats—can be found in large parts of Africa and Asia.

NORTH AMERICA

ATLANTIC

PACIFIC OCEAN

SOUTH AMERICA

EXPLORERS' CORNER

Some big cats are experts at camouflaging themselves, so they can sneak up on prey. (We should know; sometimes we've had to spend days in the bush waiting for a glimpse.) Consequently, counting them is not an easy task. Experts don't know exactly how many of each species remain in the wild. But scientists can make well-informed guesses, and they're not pretty. Over the past century, humans have relentlessly hunted big cats, causing their numbers to drop. Humans have also converted big cat habitats into homes, businesses, and farmland, which has left many of these animals without a place to rest their paws.

JAGUARS

This big cat lives in dense forest habitat where it is hard to find. For this reason, it has been difficult for scientists to estimate the size of the jaguar population.

LEOPARDS

While the leopards have the most extensive range of the big cats, their numbers are believed to be falling, too. Clashes with humans and illegal hunting have taken a toll on this species.

TIGERS

Of all the big cats, tigers face the gravest risk of extinction. Only a few thousand are believed to live in the wild. Governments around the world are working together to save them.

LIONS

In the 1800s, millions of these cats ranged throughout Africa and Asia. Today, only a fraction of this number remains. Experts are hard at work to stop the decline of the lion population.

EUROPE

ASIA

AFRICA

PACIFIC OCEAN

INDIAN OCEAN

OCEAN

AUSTRALIA

ANTARCTICA

MAP KEY
For the Approximate Ranges of Four Big Cats

- Jaguar
- Lion
- Tiger
- Leopard
- Leopard and Lion
- Leopard and Tiger

SCALE AT THE EQUATOR

0 — 2,000 miles

0 — 2,000 kilometers

CATNIP THERE ARE MORE TIGERS IN CAPTIVITY IN THE UNITED STATES ALONE THAN IN THE WILD THROUGHOUT THE WORLD.

LIGER
MALE LION + FEMALE TIGER

This super-size offspring inherits Mom's stripes, Dad's shaggy mane, and a tendency to grow to gigantic proportions. Ligers can weigh almost as much as a lion and tiger combined. The world record holder for the biggest cat is a liger named Hercules. He was 12 feet long and tipped the scales at 900 pounds! The colossal cats look amazing, but their bulky frames and risk of health problems usually give them a short life expectancy.

MIXED SIGNALS

One reason tigers and lions don't mate in the wild is they have very different mating signals. Tigers are solitary, spending most of their time avoiding one another and sticking to their own territories. They signal a readiness to mate by spraying urine or other fluids around an area. Lions, on the other hand, are the social butterflies of the cat kingdom. They live in large groups and communicate with a range of social cues. A lioness might paw at the jaw of a prospective mate or brush her head against his.

CATNIP   A LION'S TOP RUNNING SPEED IS 36 MILES PER HOUR.

BIG CAT COMBO

WHILE THE NUMBER
OF WILD BIG CATS IS DECLINING, THEIR NUMBERS IN CAPTIVITY ARE ON THE RISE.
Many zoos and parks try very hard to give big cats homes that feel as natural as possible. Occasionally, however, big cat keepers experiment with unnatural cat combinations. The result: Cat hybrids that wouldn't exist in the wild.

The most popular cat combos happen when tigers and lions are bred together. In nature, a tiger and a lion would be an odd couple and they wouldn't mate. Their offspring's mismatched genes would make the cubs vulnerable to health problems such as blindness, deafness, and heart problems. That's why most scientists think these peculiar pairings aren't a good idea.

TIGON
MALE TIGER + FEMALE LION

This cat crossing results in average-size offspring outfitted with stripes, and, on males, a mini-mane. Tigons normally grow no larger than their parents. These hybrids are not as common as ligers (perhaps because they don't grow up to be giants). Unfortunately, tigons are vulnerable to the same health problems that plague ligers.

It's no yawning matter. These ligers have no way of knowing that their very existence is controversial.

A PHOTOGRAPHIC DIAGRAM

BIG CATS UP CLOSE

BIG CATS ARE DESIGNED
TO BE FAST, INTELLIGENT, AND POWERFUL.
They need these qualities to be successful hunters. Here are some of the features that give big cats their feline superpowers.

Long tails help big cats balance while leaping, climbing, and running. They're also used to communicate.

Sheaths at the top of each toe protect claws as sharp as knife points. In big cats, the claws retract, or move back into, the sheaths when the animals aren't using them.

Long muscular legs allow big cats to jump long distances and take big strides while running.

Fur coats protect big cats' sensitive body parts, shelter them from nasty weather, and provide camouflage in their home environments.

A Bengal tiger shows off an impressive physique as it sprints for its supper.

A rounded head encloses a brain that is large in relation to big cats' body size. Cats need a lot of brainpower to outsmart prey.

Eyes have an extra layer of light-absorbing cells. This feature allows cats to see six times better at night than humans do.

Long canine teeth are used to stab prey.

A big cat nose has more than 100 million scent-sensing cells. That's 20 times more smelling power than humans have.

A flexible spine allows cats to make quick twists and turns during high-speed chases. It also helps cats land on their feet if they tumble from a high perch.

Ears can detect many sounds that humans would never notice. Cats can even tell by listening when disasters like earthquakes and volcanic eruptions are about to occur.

Sensitive whiskers help cats find their way in the dark and squeeze in and out of tight spaces.

LIFE
OF A
BIG CAT

Female lions and cubs wade through floodwaters of the Okavango Delta in Botswana.

A leopard mother gently gives her cub a lift.

BRINGING UP BABY

A tigress licks one of her cubs. Licking cleans the newborn and establishes an important bond between mother and cub.

BIG CATS MIGHT RULE
THEIR TERRITORY, BUT THEY DON'T START
OUT THAT WAY. At birth, cubs are blind and helpless. Big cats usually have between two and four cubs per litter. Just as with human babies, caring for cubs is a full-time job. Big cats are mammals, so mothers must nurse cubs for several months. Then, the cubs move on to meat meals. When a big cat has multiple mouths to feed, she has to hunt more frequently.

Moms must protect cubs from predators such as hyenas, baboons, and other big cats. They move their babies frequently to keep enemies off guard. To do this, mothers gently lift cubs by loose skin on their necks. Cubs relax their muscles and hang quietly. Wigglers would feel a pinch.

Cubs stay under their mothers' care for up to two years. During this time, cubs have a lot to learn. Their mother teaches them the best hunting locations and strategies. They learn which animals are dangerous and which make a good meal. They find out where the safest resting places and watering holes are. It's like Big Cat University and Mom's the professor!

Legadema

Two lion cubs roughhouse with their mother.

EXPLORERS' CORNER

What do you do when a fearless leopard cub crawls into the front seat of your jeep? We had this experience while we were filming and photographing in Botswana. A courageous cub, called Legadema (pronounced LOCK-ah-DEE-ma), became used to our presence. She would lie in the cool shadow of our jeep, while her mom was off hunting. One day, she jumped onto the passenger seat, like a dog going for a ride. We wanted to discourage this behavior, which could get her into trouble with tourists or, worse, poachers. Dereck tried to teach her some manners the way her mother would; he hissed at her. She ignored him. So we turned on the jeep's heater, which made a louder noise. She got the message.

We returned to the area after Legadema had grown up and had cubs of her own. It didn't take long before she was lounging in the shade of our jeep, just like she used to. We had made a friend for life.

CATNIP LARGE CATS' OFFSPRING ARE CALLED CUBS, WHILE SMALL CATS' YOUNGSTERS ARE KNOWN AS KITTENS.

ALONE ON THE PROWL

Tigers tend to hunt and patrol their territory solo.

A solitary jaguar pads through the grass.

MOST CATS PREFER THE SINGLE LIFE.

USUALLY, BIG CATS ONLY TOLERATE COMPANY IN ORDER TO

mate or to raise their cubs. Big cats communicate with scent marks or roars to let their neighbors know, "This is my space. Keep out!"

But there's one big exception: lions. Lions are the only cats that live in social groups, called prides. Within a pride, nearly every female is related. Moms, sisters, aunts, and cousins all work together to raise cubs and hunt for enough food to support the pride. A dominant male or two will guard the pride's territory. He also babysits the cubs while their mothers are off hunting.

Young males are forced to leave the pride once they are old enough to hunt for themselves. These lions sometimes form small, all-boy gangs, called bachelor groups. The youngsters stay together until they're big enough to challenge a dominant male for control of a pride.

...OR THE MORE THE MERRIER?

LION AROUND

A LION'S TO-DO LIST

Snoozing	16 hours a day
Hunting for food	2 hours
Grooming and socializing	1 hour and 10 minutes
Eating	50 minutes

A pride's lionesses turn raising cubs into a group effort.

WHAT'S FOR LUNCH?

There's no fast food in the places where big cats live, but there is food that moves fast. Big cats have to work to snag their supper. Here are some of the favorite hard-earned meals in their diet.

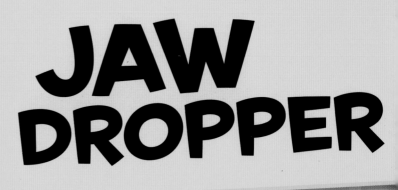

JAGUAR

Fish A favorite dish; jaguars will dive right into water to catch a seafood meal.

Small crocodiles Large crocs are too dangerous to tangle with, but smaller crocodiles yield tasty meat and are worth the risk.

Peccarries These pig-like animals of North and South America are another jaguar favorite.

TIGER

Chital Deer This spotted deer is native to Asia and is popular tiger prey.

Sambar Deer This is another deer that is a common meal for tigers.

Water Buffalo Tigers' most challenging quarry, water buffalo will charge and have been known to injure and even kill tigers.

LION

Zebras If a lion can separate a young or sick zebra from the herd, it will gladly take this striped snack.

Wildebeests This variety of antelope is another popular choice for lions.

Cape Buffalo This animal is dangerous prey for lions, but some strictly prefer this meaty prize.

LEOPARD

Impalas These speedy antelopes are common prey for leopards.

Monkeys Leopards already lounge in trees, so they might as well hunt there, too. A quick leopard can snag a vervet monkey off its guard.

Porcupines This prickly snack can only be hunted very carefully, unless the leopard wants a muzzle full of spines.

CATS CAN'T LIVE OFF

PLANTS, SO THEY MUST HUNT FOR EVERYTHING THEY EAT. Cats usually stalk their prey by crouching low to the ground and silently sneaking up on it. When the moment is right, the cat will strike. It leaps on to the prey, baring sharp fangs and claws. Sometimes cats will chase their prey for short distances. Oftentimes, a cat's efforts will fail and its potential prey escapes. The cat will go hungry until a hunt is successful.

Even though big cats use hunting strategies that aren't for the faint of heart, these top predators actually make their habitat healthier. In fact, big cats serve a very important role in the ecosystem. Cats such as lions and tigers keep the numbers of plant-eating animals in check, so plants have a chance to grow and thrive. They also keep grazing herds healthier by picking off sick and wounded members. Without big cats, delicate ecosystems would be out of balance.

STEAK DINNER

Tigers can eat more than 80 pounds (36 kg) of meat in one sitting. That's the equivalent of about 70 T-bone steaks!

CATNIP A LEOPARD CAN DRAG PREY AS HIGH AS 50 FEET (15 METERS) UP A TREE—EVEN IF ITS MEAL IS LARGER AND HEAVIER THAN ITSELF!

Female lions team up to bring down a Cape buffalo.

BIG CATS' HUNTING METHODS
MAY SEEM HARSH TO US,
BUT THEY'RE JUST DOING WHAT THEY NEED TO DO IN ORDER TO EAT.

A leopard heaves a heavy impala up a tree.

A tiger crouches low to the ground in an attempt to make a stealthy strike.

CLASHING
WITH BIG CATS

Amazon rain forest trees are chopped down and burned in Brazil.

EVERY BIG CAT SHARES
ONE BIG PROBLEM: HABITAT LOSS.
AS HUMAN POPULATIONS GROW, PEOPLE
take over land for homes, businesses, and farms. This leaves fewer wild places for animals. To cope with their shrinking world, big cats sometimes prey on valuable livestock. This upsets farmers because livestock are often the only way of supporting their families. As a consequence, some feline offenders are shot or poisoned.

CATNIP SOMETIMES BIG CATS ARE POACHED FOR THEIR BODY PARTS, SUCH AS SKIN, WHISKERS, TEETH, AND BONES.

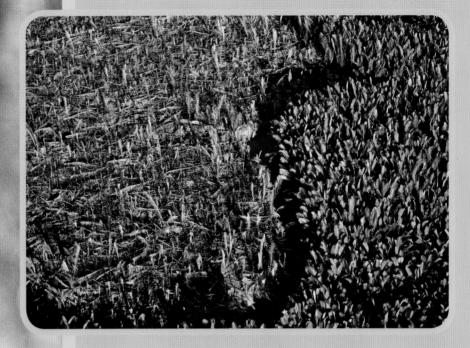

The majority of mangrove forests in Indonesia's Mahakam Delta were cut down due to shrimp farming.

A Bengal tiger rests in a tangle of mangrove trees in Bangladesh.

Disappearing Habitats

3 tiger subspecies have become extinct in the past century.

300 Asiatic lions remain in the Gir Forest in India. This subspecies of lion is almost extinct.

1/2 of jaguars' natural habitat has been lost over the last hundred years.

45 Amur leopards, an Asian subspecies, are probably all that remain in the wild. This leopard is one of the world's rarest cats.

Can humans and big cats live together peacefully? Many people think they can; it just might take extra effort on our part. In some areas, wildlife conservationists pay farmers for lost livestock, so long as they don't kill big cats. Conservationists also teach farmers ways to keep livestock safe, such as building pens with metal fences and keeping wild pigs (which attract cats) out of crops.

In many countries, governments have set aside large areas of land as reserves. There, animals are protected from habitat loss and hunting. Animal-related tourism such as safaris may help big cats, too. Travelers pay money to see big cats up close. Local people who work at lodges and tour companies make money. For them, this makes big cats more valuable alive than dead—and worth protecting.

A PHOTO GALLERY

ALL THE CATS

BIG CATS MAKE UP
ONLY 4 OF THE 36 SPECIES OF CATS.

These other cats may not be as large, but they're still feared hunters in their habitats. Keen senses, sharp claws, and pointed teeth give all cats an edge in the search for prey.

A caracal has distinctive tufts of long, black hair on its ears. Fittingly, the name comes from a Turkish word meaning "black eared."

The territorial ocelot can be found in North and South America. It is also known as a painted leopard.

The elusive Asiatic golden cat mainly lives in forests and is rarely seen.

The shy, nocturnal marbled cat lives in thick forests of Southeast Asia.

A serval uses its big ears to tune into the sounds of scurrying prey.

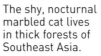

A fast cheetah keeps a sharp lookout.

Half the size of a house cat, the rusty spotted cat is a pint-size feline. Most members of the species can be found only on the island of Sri Lanka.

One-month-old Pallas Cat kittens hiss for the camera.

A sand cat lives in the deserts of North Africa and the Middle East. It gets most of its water from its food.

The Canada lynx has a short, bobbed tail tipped with black fur.

3
BEYOND THE BIG CAT

A bobcat descends a rocky slope in Colorado. These feisty cats can only be found in North America. Bobcats are one of four species of lynx.

CAT FAMILY TREE

Paramachairodus

Metailurus

Proailurnus

Pseudaelurus

ALL CATS, FROM THE MIGHTY TIGER TO THE COMMON HOUSE CAT, EVOLVED FROM A SMALL,

catlike creature that lived 12 million years ago. Eventually, the feline family split into two types. One branch grew into the smaller cats such as pumas, lynx, and domestic cats. The big cats sprang out of the other branch. Today's domestic cats are actually big cats' cousins. Cats really are one big family!

SMALL CAT, TALL CAT

One of the smallest living cats is the teacup-sized domestic breed Singapura. Its towering cousin, the Siberian tiger, is the largest living cat. One of the biggest cats to ever exist was the American cave lion. It may have tipped the scales at 1,100 pounds (500 kg).

36.5–23.5 MILLION YEARS AGO	23.5–5.3 MILLION YEARS AGO

Machairodus

Homotherium

Smilodon

Megantereon

Dinofelis

Leopardus

Puma

Felis

Miracinonyx

Acinonyx

Panthera

A MOUTHY RELATIVE

With two dagger-like teeth that didn't even fit inside their mouths, saber-toothed cats might be felines' most infamous ancestor. Several of these long-fanged species lived between 2.5 million and 10,000 years ago. The cats' canine teeth grew up to 7 inches (18 centimeters) long. The fangs had one drawback: such long teeth were prone to breaking. To protect them, saber-toothed cats didn't grab prey with their mouths. They pinned their prey down with sharp claws and strong paws. Then, the cats used their teeth to slash their victims.

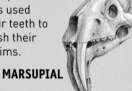

MARSUPIAL

NIMRAVID

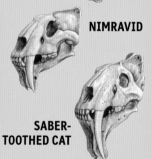

SABER-TOOTHED CAT

A wide-set jaw with dagger-like fangs evolved independently in some unrelated animals. Marsupials (pouched animals), an extinct meat eater called nimravid, and cats all sported the tapered teeth at some point in history.

This thick-furred cat pads through the snow with giant paws that act like snowshoes.

CANADA LYNX

CATNIP CHEETAHS CAN REACH SPEEDS UP TO 70 MPH (112 KPH) IN LESS THAN THREE SECONDS, FASTER THAN A RACE CAR CAN ACCELERATE.

NOT-SO-BIG CATS

BIG CATS MIGHT HAVE SIZE

ON THEIR SIDE, BUT WHEN IT COMES DOWN TO THE NUMBERS, SMALL CATS HAVE THEM BEAT.

Most cats in the feline family tree belong to the small-cat branch. These cats have a different throat structure from big cats. They can't roar, but they have a different ability. Smaller cats can purr continually. Small cats can be found in almost any environment on Earth—from the desert-dwelling sand cat to the rain forest–residing margay. Cats such as the Canada lynx can even brave bone-chilling winters in the northern tundra.

Classifying cats isn't always clear-cut. Snow leopards have the same throat structure as big cats but have never been known to roar. Pumas are usually classified with small cats—they don't roar either. But these super-sized kitties can weigh up to 230 pounds (104 kg), more than an average leopard.

Cheetahs aren't closely related to either big or small cats. They descend from a line of running cats and are the last of their kind. Body features such as extra-long legs, a long spine, and claws that work like runner's spikes allow these cats to hold the title of world's fastest land animal.

Crouching low, the caracal stalks birds and rodents in short savanna grass.

CARACAL

PALLAS CAT

This cat hunts during the day when its prey is most active.

The largest of the "small cats," the puma has a giant range that stretches from the tip of South America to the top of the Canadian Rockies.

PUMA

LISTEN TO THE CATS!
A ROAR OR PURR INDICATES BIG CAT OR SMALLER COUSIN.

WILD CAT

HUNTING HEAVYWEIGHTS

Many wild cats can take down prey that are often more than twice their size.

TRY, TRY AGAIN

For many types of wild cats, only a small portion of hunting attempts are successful. About 10 to 20 percent of tiger hunts end in a kill.

SMELLY MESSAGES

Many wild cat species prominently mark their territory with urine and droppings.

MANY SPECIES

Scientists have tallied 35 species of wild cats in the world.

NOT FIT FOR LIVING ROOMS

Keeping wild cats as pets is a dangerous idea. Wild cats have complex needs that are best met in their natural environment. They can seriously injure or kill people when handled incorrectly.

TAME TABBY

STICKING WITH SMALL SNACKS

Domestic cats often hunt pint-sized critters such as mice, birds, and lizards.

HOTSHOT HUNTERS

Domestic cats can be very efficient hunters. At the top of their game, one in three attempts results in a kill.

DISCREETLY DOING THEIR BUSINESS

Domestic cats neatly bury their droppings.

ONE SPECIES, MANY BREEDS

Domestic cats all belong to a single species (*Felis catus*), but they come in more than 80 breeds.

PERFECT PETS

Domestic cats have been living with humans for 9,000 years and are practiced companions for many people.

CATNIP THERE ARE APPROXIMATELY 93.6 MILLION PET CATS IN THE UNITED STATES.

CAT CARE

Zoo cats often receive a lot of hands-on care to keep them fit and healthy, including a teeth cleaning!

WITH THEIR STRENGTH AND BEAUTY, WILD CATS HAVE STAR POWER AMONG HUMAN ADMIRERS. VISITORS TO ZOOS AND

wildlife parks often scramble to see cat exhibits. Zoos allow millions of people to get close to animals they would likely never see in the wild. With expert care, zoos and animal parks can provide environments that help captive cats feel at home.

Most zoos use techniques called animal enrichment that help animals tap into their natural instincts. Zoo animals spend their days in the same enclosure. This could get very boring for intelligent animals like big cats. So how do you help a lion in a city zoo feel like it's prowling the African savanna? Keepers can stuff a cardboard "zebra" with meat or scatter antelope dung in the lions' enclosure. Interaction with scents and sights of prey animals allow the cats to act like their wild counterparts.

Zookeepers also train cats to follow commands such as come, sit, stand, and lie down. Training gives cats a mental workout. It also allows veterinarians to visually check out the animals without resorting to drugs to make them sleepy.

FOR THE FIRST SIX WEEKS OF THEIR LIVES, YOUNG CUBS CAN FEED UP TO EIGHT TIMES A DAY.

YOU BE THE ZOOKEEPER

Many pet owners often practice animal enrichment without even knowing it. Like zoo animals, pets thrive in environments where they get to use their instincts and smarts. How can you help a pet cat connect with its wild side? Provide safe, pet-friendly toys and change them frequently. Challenge your cat with interesting scents like catnip. Use treats as food rewards for good behavior or create food puzzles, like treats in an empty open water bottle.

A white
tiger cub
drinks milk
from a
bottle.

CATNIP ZOO SCIENTISTS HAVE DEVELOPED A DRUG THAT ALLOWS FIELD RESEARCHERS TO SEDATE AND SAFELY FIT WILD TIGERS WITH RADIO COLLARS.

YOU DON'T
HAVE TO ROAR WHEN YOU'RE ANGRY OR

purr when you're content to have some things in common with cats. Both humans and cats are mammals. That means both nurse their young with milk, have body hair, and are warm blooded. Let's see some other ways big cats compare with your world.

CAT COMPARISONS
CHANNELING YOUR INNER CAT

Young children have 20 teeth. Human teeth are shaped for a mixed diet of plants and meat. Lions and tigers have 30 teeth. Their large stabbing teeth, called canines, are used to catch and kill prey.

SLEEPING

It's no coincidence that "catnap" is a term for sleep. Cats are experts at getting their zzz's. By sleeping in short stretches at a time, cats sleep as many as 20 hours a day. Most kids sleep for about 9 or 10 hours a night. But while a leopard snoozes in a tree, you likely prefer a comfy bed.

STRETCHING

Your gym teacher may have you stretch before a workout to keep your muscles flexible. Cats stretch for similar reasons. But for them, no yoga mat is required.

GROOMING

You likely need a brush or comb to tame your strands. Big cats have a brush built in to their tongues! A cat's tongue is covered with backward-facing spines that act like bristles. Cats lick their fur to remove loose hair and dead skin.

NAIL CARE

You probably trim your nails with nail clippers. Big cats need something more heavy-duty for their sharp, curved claws. To keep their nails sharp and clean, big cats dig their claws into a tree, flex them, and pull down.

During playtime, a leopard cub toys with its mother as the pair rests in the shade.

4

FUN
WITH
BIG CATS

CATCH A CAT—
IF YOU CAN!

EACH SPECIES
OF BIG CAT HAS A UNIQUE

cat pattern. This camouflage helps the cat blend into its environment. Cats would go hungry if their prey were able to spot them easily and escape. Do you have what it takes to spot big cats? Put your skills to the test. How many big cats can you find on this page?

WHAT'S YOUR CAT PURR-SONALITY?

HAVE YOU EVER

WONDERED WHAT TYPE of feline you would be? Take this quiz to find out!

1 **What type of meal sounds the most delicious to you?**
- **A.** An extra-large steak, the rarer the better
- **B.** Sharing a family-style supper
- **C.** Chowing down while perched on a high countertop
- **D.** Nibbling on several small snacks throughout the day

2 **Which statement best describes your approach to social interactions?**
- **A.** I'm a loner and most comfortable by myself.
- **B.** The more the merrier; I like to hang out with big groups.
- **C.** I'm solitary, but I don't mind when others come into my space.
- **D.** I prefer to be around only a couple of my favorite folks.

3 **Where is your perfect living spot?**
- **A.** No preference. I'll live where it's hot or cold.
- **B.** I like sunny grasslands.
- **C.** I like warm, wooded places such as jungles and forests.
- **D.** I just want to be indoors!

4 **What do you like to wear?**
- **A.** Stripes
- **B.** Solid colors
- **C.** Spots
- **D.** A variety of patterns

5 **What describes your approach to physical fitness?**
- **A.** I focus on strength and power.
- **B.** I need both power and speed.
- **C.** I concentrate on flexibility and power.
- **D.** I aim to be fast and graceful.

CATNIP LION CUBS ARE BORN SPOTTED FOR EXTRA CAMOUFLAGE AS THEY HIDE IN THE BUSH. THESE SPOTS MOSTLY FADE BY ADULTHOOD.

WHAT'S YOUR PLACE IN THE FELINE FAMILY?

IF YOU SCORED MOSTLY A's: You're like the mighty tiger. A solitary yet powerful force, you're comfortable in a variety of environments.

IF YOU SCORED MOSTLY B's: You're like the majestic lion. At ease in a crowd, you like to use your power and speed to race through sunny savannas.

IF YOU SCORED MOSTLY C's: You're like the stealthy leopard. You're not strictly territorial, but you're no social butterfly either. You often sport your spots in steamy climates.

IF YOU SCORED MOSTLY D's: You're like the cunning house cat. Ever resourceful, you like to cuddle up with your favorite humans and take advantage of easy meals.

PHYSICAL FEATS

A large tiger can leap more than **30 FEET** (9.1 meters) to pounce on its prey. That's about the length of three mini-vans parked in a row.

BIG CATS USE MUSCULAR LEGS AND

a superb sense of balance to leap extraordinary distances. If animals were allowed in the Olympics, big cats could definitely compete in the jumping events. Which cat would likely take first prize in the long jump?

JUMPING CONTEST

How far can you jump compared to big cats? Use a tape measure to see how you measure up against these four-legged jumping champs. Just remember, what goes up must come down. Be sure to practice your jumping safely and on level ground.

Jumping contestants not to scale.

5 FEET   **10 FEET**   **15 FEET**

Lions can jump up to
36 FEET
(11 meters). They can clear the length of a school bus in a single bound.

GOLD MEDAL WINNER!

Snow leopards are able to soar through the air as far as
45 FEET
(14 meters)—the length of a humpback whale. They have to be champion leapers to hunt among the cliffs and ravines of their mountainous home.

Jaguars and leopards are able to leap
20 FEET
(6 meters). That's the height of many two-story buildings!

MORE COOL CAT TRICKS

In one stride, a cheetah can cover up to
26 FEET
(7–8 meters).

Tigers are capable swimmers and divers. They can swim across lakes while dragging heavy prey in their mouths.

Leopards are the strongest climbers of the cats. They can carry prey twice their weight up a tree.

CATNIP BIG CATS HAVE THE BEST 3-D VISION OF ALL CARNIVORES, WHICH HELPS THEM CORRECTLY GAUGE DISTANCES WHILE JUMPING.

20 FEET   25 FEET   30 FEET   35 FEET   40 FEET   45 FEET

CATS IN CULTURE

HUMANS HAVE RESPECTED CATS' IMPRESSIVE LOOKS AND PHYSICAL ABILITIES FOR THOUSANDS OF YEARS.

Some cultures even believed cats had supernatural powers. The Maya, a Central American people, believed a powerful jaguar god guided the dead to the afterlife. For ancient Romans, some gods rode atop great cats or used felines to pull their chariots. The Egyptians believed cats were so sacred that they carefully mummified their bodies while the whole family mourned their death.

Cats' reputation among humans, however, wasn't always positive. During the late Middle Ages, large numbers of cats were killed because people believed cats were associated with witchcraft and evil. Cats had a tough time again in the early Renaissance period, when the Christian church wanted to stamp out reminders of a cat-related pagan symbol.

Today, most people don't believe in feline superstitions, such as black cats causing bad luck. Now, many humans accept cats for what they are—animals that are just trying to survive in a changing world.

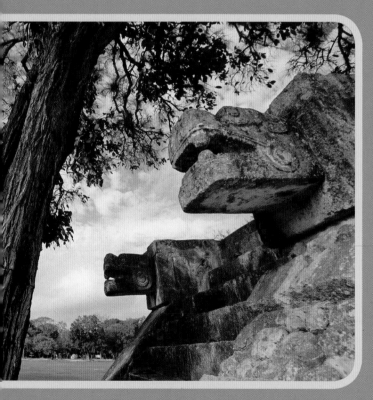

Giant carved jaguar heads adorn a Maya temple in Mexico.

Many ancient Egyptians believed cats represented the goddess Bastet. Dead cats were often mummified in preparation for the afterlife.

CATNIP   THE BENGAL TIGER IS INDIA'S NATIONAL ANIMAL.

SEEING LIONS IN STARS

Ancient stargazers believed a constellation—or patch of stars—looked like a lion. They named it "Leo," the Greek word for lion. People born under the astrological sign Leo are said to have lion-like qualities: pride, bravery, strength, and arrogance.

MAKE YOUR OWN CATNIP

Catnip is an herb that's been used for centuries as a treat for cats. The plant, which is related to mint, contains a chemical that attracts some cats like crazy. To have a fresh supply for your cat, you can grow your own catnip. Plant catnip seeds in a sunny area and water them daily. After the plant grows several inches, pinch off budding leaves and lay them out to dry. Crumple the leaves and sew them into a felt pouch to make a mouse toy for your cat.

In this 180 A.D. mosaic, the Greek god Dionysus is pictured riding a leopard.

PHOTO FINISH

BEHIND THE SHOT WITH BEVERLY JOUBERT

FILMMAKERS
AND PHOTOGRAPHERS

who follow big cats all share one goal: to let people to see these animals from the safety of their television sets or the pages of books and magazines. They wish to share the cats' fierce beauty and fascinating behaviors with the world. It's a noble undertaking, but it's not easy.

Most photographers and filmmakers crave adventure. In places where big cats live, there's plenty of that to go around. Beverly and Dereck Joubert film and photograph leopards and lions in Botswana. Most days, they sleep in tents and bathe in crocodile-infested rivers. Every morning, they have to shake out their shoes (in case a scorpion snuck in) and double lock their tent zippers (in case baboons try to get in). The midday heat climbs to a scorching 128°F (53°C), while overnight temperatures plunge to below freezing. Sometimes, things can get too exciting if a cranky elephant or startled lion mounts a charge. Misjudging either the weather or the wildlife can be a fatal mistake.

But when the filmmakers get the perfect shot of a lion hunt or capture the gaze of a leopard's wild, golden eyes, they don't want to be anywhere else.

CANDID CAPTURE!
A lion cub hangs from a tree in Botswana.

AFTERWORD

LIVING WITH BIG CATS

AS THE HUMAN
POPULATION SOARS, BIG CATS'

numbers have tumbled worldwide. There is a chance these felines are going the way of the saber-tooth, yet this time, humankind would be responsible. But don't count out big cats yet! Some of the world's most respected biologists are on the case. Advances in the methods of studying big cats have led to a more accurate understanding of cat biology and population estimates. While the numbers currently look grim, many experts see signs of hope. And armed with accurate information, conservationists know the best places to focus their efforts.

In Central and South America, conservationists are working with governments to connect fragmented pieces of jaguar habitat. Safe routes between these wild places mean jaguars can breed and hunt throughout their range, even though humans live in large parts of it. Clear paths for jaguar migration can help ensure the big cat remains genetically strong and diverse.

In Southeast Asia, scientists have identified vast areas of healthy tiger habitat. There is enough wild land and prey to support an estimated 15,000 to 20,000 tigers. Community reforestation projects in Nepal are creating tiger habitat out of previously cleared land. If the world's remaining tigers can be protected, there are areas where they can thrive and rebound.

In Africa, ecotourism is helping local people make a living from showing off big cats in action. Simple changes in farming and ranching practices can keep livestock safe from big cats. Plus, new projects like the

Conflict between lions and the Maasai people of eastern Africa have contributed to cats' decreasing numbers in Kenya and Tanzania. With herding as their means of survival, Maasai warriors feel forced to retaliate against cats when a tribe's livestock has been attacked.

Mbirikani Predator Compensation Fund offer herding tribes immediate compensation for cattle lost to hunting lions. This reduces the chance of people killing the cats for threatening their livelihood.

Big cats have been around for hundreds of thousands of years. They are adaptable, intelligent, and tough. Plus, they reproduce quickly. Tigers, for example, can produce a litter of cubs every year. This means cats' numbers can rebound quickly under the right conditions. With a little bit of help, big cats just might have a few of their "nine lives" left.

If you would like to help, visit http://animals.nationalgeographic.com/animals/big-cats **for more information.**

BIG CAT INITIATIVE

THE NATIONAL GEOGRAPHIC SOCIETY HAS HEARD the desperate roar of the big cat community. To help lions, tigers, leopards, jaguars, and the world's other large felines, National Geographic launched the Big Cat Initiative. This program aims to stop the free fall of lion population numbers by 2015. Eventually, it hopes to bring lion numbers back to healthy levels. But that's not all. Through conservation projects, education, and spreading the word about the big cats' plight, the Big Cat Initiative hopes to ensure the long-term survival of all big cats. The program is working to involve local people in the regions where cats live. That way, the communities in direct contact with cats have an important role to play.

A veterinarian listens to a sedated African lion's heartbeat at a Namibian wildlife park.

A lion mother and cub watch the sun rise at the dawn of a new day.

AN INTERACTIVE GLOSSARY

Female lions lounge in the mud. The bond between these pride members is strong.

THESE WORDS ARE
COMMONLY USED AMONG BIG CAT experts.

Use the glossary to see what each word means and go to page numbers listed to see the word used in context. Then test your big cat smarts!

1. Adaptation
(PAGES 10-11)
An evolutionary change in an animal or plant that helps it live in a particular environment.

Which adaptation helps big cats hunt well in the dark?
a. long fangs
b. long legs and sharp claws
c. spotted or striped coats
d. extra light-sensing cells in their eyes

2. Camouflage
(PAGES 18-19, 46-47)
A body shape or coloring that conceals animals from predators or prey

What is the main reason big cats use camouflage?
a. to signal other animals
b. to be more successful hunters
c. to attract mates
d. all of the above

3. Carnivore
(PAGES 10-11, 26-27)
An animal that eats the flesh of other animals

What kind of teeth would you expect a carnivore to have?
a. sharp and pointy
b. square and flat
c. a mix of sharp and flat teeth
d. no teeth, only gums

4. Conservationist
(PAGES 28-29, 56-57)
A person who works to protect and manage Earth's natural resources and the wildlife that depends on those resources

What quality would be important for a person who wants to be a conservationist?
a. likes to work outside
b. good at communicating with people
c. likes to work with animals
d. all of the above

5. Diet
(PAGES 26-27)
The foods eaten by a particular group of animals

Which is part of a leopard's diet?
a. cat food
b. tater tots
c. small forest animals
d. scrub grass

6. Dominant
(PAGES 24-25)
The status of being an animal that exerts authority and control over other animals in a group

A dominant lion might exhibit which behavior?
a. backing off when another cat challenges it
b. fighting other cats for the juiciest pieces of a kill
c. letting other cats mate with members of the pride
d. all of the above

7. Ecosystem
(PAGES 6-7)
All the living things in a community and the environment in which they live

A lion can share an ecosystem with which animal?
a. leopards
b. Cape buffalo
c. zebras
d. all of the above

8. Gene
(PAGES 12-13, 16-17)
A unit of hereditary information that encodes the traits passed from parents to offspring

Which jaguar feature is certain to be determined by genes?
a. taste for crocodiles
b. black fur
c. success in raising cubs to adulthood
d. all of the above

9. Mammal
(PAGES 22-23, 42-43)
A warm-blooded animal whose young feed on milk that is produced by the mother

Which of the following is a feature of mammals?
a. cold-bloodedness
b. bodies covered in scales
c. high level of maternal care
d. very successful carnivores

10. Nocturnal
(PAGE 30)
The state of being active at night

Nocturnal animals spend a lot of time sleeping ___.
a. in caves
b. in short bursts
c. in groups
d. during the day

11. Poacher
(PAGES 22-23)
A person who illegally hunts animals, usually to sell their meat, skins, or other body parts

Hunting is only considered poaching when it ___.
a. occurs at night
b. violates laws
c. results in the killing of multiple animals
d. is practiced with guns

12. Prey
(PAGES 10-11, 26-27, 46-47)
An animal that is hunted and eaten by another

Which of the following can be a jaguar's prey?
a. peccary
b. wildebeest
c. impala
d. chital deer

13. Predator
(pages 6-7)
An animal that hunts and eats other animals

Which of the following would a predator not eat?
a. wheat
b. deer
c. porcupines
d. monkeys

14. Pride
(PAGES 24-25)
A group of lions

A lion pride is generally made up of ___.
a. young males
b. an equal number of males and females
c. related females
d. cubs

15. Reserve
(PAGES 28-29)
A tract of public land set apart for conservation purposes

Which of the following activities would probably not be allowed in a reserve?
a. camping
b. sightseeing
c. logging
d. hiking

ANSWERS: 1. d, **2.** b, **3.** a, **4.** d, **5.** c, **6.** b, **7.** d, **8.** b, **9.** c, **10.** d, **11.** b, **12.** a, **13.** a, **14.** c, **15.** c.

Amur leopards, like this one, are the world's rarest big cats.

FIND OUT MORE

BOOKS AND ARTICLES

Face to Face With Leopards.
Dereck Joubert and Beverly Joubert
National Geographic Children's Books, AUGUST 2009.
Face to Face With Lions.
Dereck Joubert and Beverly Joubert
National Geographic Children's Books, MARCH 2010.
"Leopards: Nature's Supercats"
Crispin Boyer, *National Geographic Kids.*
Washington, D.C.: MAY 2009.
"Path of the Jaguar"
Mel White, *National Geographic.* Washington, D.C.:
MARCH 2009.
Mountain Lions.
Erika L. Shores, Capstone Press. Bloomington,
MN: AUGUST 2010.
Cheetahs.
Deborah Nuzzolo, Pebble Plus. Bloomington,
MN: FEBRUARY 2010.
Big Cats (Xtreme Predators).
S. L. Hamilton, Abdo Publishing Company.
Edina, MN: JANUARY 2010.
Big Cats: Wild Reads.
Kenneth Ireland, Oxford University Press, USA.
New York: OCTOBER 2009.

MOVIES TO WATCH

"Eye of the Leopard"
National Geographic. Washington, D.C.: FEBRUARY 2007
"Tigers of the Snow"
National Geographic. Washington, D.C.: FEBRUARY 2000
"In Search of the Jaguar"
National Geographic. Washington, D.C.: OCTOBER 2006

WEB SITES

National Geographic Big Cats Initiative
This program works to help ensure that there is enough land
and resources for both humans AND big cats.
http://animals.nationalgeographic.com/animals/big-cats/

WWF's Tiger Initiative
To mark 2010 as the Year of the Tiger, the WWF launched a
new campaign to save the most endangered of big cats.
**http://wwf.panda.org/what_we_do/endangered_species/
tigers/tiger_initiative/**

Panthera
This conservation organization is dedicated to protecting the
world's 36 species of wild cats. **http://www.panthera.org/**

PLACES TO VISIT

The most exciting way to learn about big cats is to see them
yourself! Find out if your local zoo or wildlife park has a big cat
exhibit. Here are a few where visitors can "roar" with delight.

San Diego Zoo's Africa Rocks (Big Cat), San Diego, California
Smithsonian National Zoo's Great Cats Exhibit, Washington, D.C.
The Bronx Zoo's Tiger Mountain, Bronx, New York
Pittsburgh Zoo's Asian Forest, Pittsburgh, Pennsylvania
Oklahoma City Zoo's Cat Forest, Oklahoma City, Oklahoma

For those who work tirelessly to ensure the survival of the world's wild cats—EC

Published by the National Geographic Society
John M. Fahey, Jr., *President and Chief Executive Officer*
Gilbert M. Grosvenor, *Chairman of the Board*
Tim T. Kelly, President, *Global Media Group*
John Q. Griffin, *Executive Vice President;*
    President, Publishing
Nina D. Hoffman, *Executive Vice President;*
    President, Book Publishing Group
Melina Gerosa Bellows, *Chief Creative Officer,*
    Kids and Family, Global Media

Prepared by the Book Division
Nancy Laties Feresten, *Vice President,*
    Editor in Chief, Children's Books
Jonathan Halling, *Design Director, Children's Publishing*
Jennifer Emmett, *Executive Editor, Children's Books*
Carl Mehler, *Director of Maps*
R. Gary Colbert, *Production Director*
Jennifer A. Thornton, *Managing Editor*

Staff for This Book
Priyanka Lamichhane, *Project Editor*
James Hiscott Jr., *Art Director*
Lori Epstein, Annette Kiesow, *Illustrations Editors*
Erin Mayes, Chad Tomlinson, *Designers*
Kate Olesin, *Editorial Assistant*
Grace Hill, *Associate Managing Editor*
Lewis R. Bassford, *Production Manager*
Susan Borke, *Legal and Business Affairs*
Madeleine Franklin, *Editorial Intern*
Janice Gilman, *Illustrations Intern*

Manufacturing and Quality Management
Christopher A. Liedel, *Chief Financial Officer*
Phillip L. Schlosser, *Senior Vice President*
Chris Brown, *Technical Director*
Nicole Elliott, *Manager*
Rachel Faulise, *Manager*
Robert L. Barr, *Manager*

Captions
Page 1: Do you think this snarling male lion looks funny or fierce?
Pages 2-3: A leopard lounges in a tree. From this perch, leopards can eat and sleep undisturbed.
Cover: A tiger splashes through the water.
Back cover: A lion yawning.

The National Geographic Society is one of the world's largest nonprofit scientific and educational organizations. Founded in 1888 to "increase and diffuse geographic knowledge," the Society works to inspire people to care about the planet. National Geographic reflects the world through its magazines, television programs, films, music and radio, books, DVDs, maps, exhibitions, live events, school publishing programs, interactive media and merchandise. *National Geographic* magazine, the Society's official journal, published in English and 32 local-language editions, is read by more than 35 million people each month. The National Geographic Channel reaches 310 million households in 34 languages in 165 countries. National Geographic Digital Media receives more than 13 million visitors a month. National Geographic has funded more than 9,200 scientific research, conservation and exploration projects and supports an education program promoting geography literacy. For more information, visit nationalgeographic.com.

For more information, please call 1-800-NGS LINE (647-5463) or write to the following address:
National Geographic Society
1145 17th Street N.W.
Washington, D.C. 20036-4688 U.S.A.

Visit us online at www.nationalgeographic.com/books

For librarians and teachers: www.ngchildrensbooks.org

More for kids from National Geographic: kids.nationalgeographic.com

For information about special discounts for bulk purchases, please contact National Geographic Books Special Sales: ngspecsales@ngs.org

For rights or permissions inquiries, please contact National Geographic Books Subsidiary Rights: ngbookrights@ngs.org

Library of Congress Cataloging-in-Publication Data
Carney, Elizabeth, 1981-
  NGK everything big cats / by Elizabeth Carney.
      p. cm.
  Includes bibliographical references and index.
  ISBN 978-1-4263-0805-5 (hardcover : alk. paper) —
  ISBN 978-1-4263-0806-2 (library binding : alk. paper)
  1. Felidae—Juvenile literature. I. Title. II. Title: Big cats.
  QL737.C23C348 2011
  599.75'5—dc22
                                          2010026963

Scholastic edition ISBN: 978-1-4263-0875-8

Printed in China
10/RRDS/1